Tiny Sliver of a Moon

Also by Mick Scott

Stardust and Scar Tissue: Rambles, Ruminations, and the Search for an Authentic Culture of Life

Tiny Sliver of a Moon

Small Poems

Mick Scott

Mick Scott
Winston-Salem, NC
Mick27101@gmail.com

First Edition

Copyright © 2024 by Mick Scott

All rights reserved, including the right of reproduction in whole or in part in any form except in the case of brief quotations embodied in critical articles or reviews. For permission, contact Mick Scott.

Cover illustration, "Flying,"
Copyright © 2024 by Mick Scott

Interior and cover layout
by Kevin Morgan Watson

ISBN: 979-8-218-53473-8

To she who brightened my days

Cool of the morning,
tiny sliver of a moon.
Put on the coffee.

I dream the arctic,
summer ermine, fox and geese,
endless light and land.

Ah, the morning light;
Tender yellow subtle stars;
Songbird alarm clock.

The sun digs its way
up from the well of winter.
Surfacing, it sighs.

Little bird outside
sings, "Diva, diva, diva!"
His morning mantra.

The bird orchestra,
This morning in my backyard.
Special guests: the crickets.

Casual bird call,
as he leans against the branch.
"Hey, girl — nice feathers."

5 a.m. runners
Like a pod of sleek dolphin
Swimming dusky streets.

In the runner's mind:
Surely this hill will get tired
long before I do.

Climbing up the hill:
Do the thing you cannot do,
Then you find you can.

The hundred-stride hill:
I ran up in ninety strides
to cheers from the crows.

Lyrical movement.
Meditation in motion.
Running/sitting still.

Honeysuckle air
As I rattle down the path.
Sunny Salem Lake.

Unexpected smiles
from a pack of biking girls
straighten my posture.

Lone old guys on bikes
Ride the trail to Salem Lake.
Someday I'll be one.

Strut like Travolta
down the middle of the street.
This is *my* city.

Summer butterflies,
Oranges, reds and yellows.
Diaphanous robes.

Two big happy dogs
Look at me expectantly.
Treats for everyone!

They say it will snow
Now, after flowers have bloomed.
The air is confused.

Cool in the morning.
Half a world away, they fight.
Sitting still is hard.

Order, disorder,
poetry and politics,
this is how it goes.

Politics today:
There will always be someone
says the earth is flat.

Little blue marble
tumbling through the galaxy
dancing the mambo.

Feeling overwhelmed?
Just sit and look at the sky.
Overwhelmed can wait.

The empire crumbles.
But grass grows between the cracks,
reaches for the sun.

In the morning room,
light filters through matchstick blinds
onto my closed eyes.

Light through the window.
Shadows like Japanese script.
Sandalwood incense.

In my dream it snowed,
flat flakes swirling past streetlights,
brilliant confetti.

I dreamed of castles,
vast dark secret passages,
then woke to flatlands.

I feel October
leaking from the other side
of the calendar.

Light is everything,
each leaf in sharp green relief,
peek of blue flowers.

It was a calm day
that slipped by despite efforts
to pay attention.

I can smell the heat.
Whiff of dust; tang of asphalt.
Miles away, it rains.

Waiting for the rain,
tense clouds hover over feet,
paddling soft flip flop.

Let the rain drop down,
let it swell the dry dirt earth,
dappled cement lot.

4 a.m. the storm.
Raindrops tapping the window;
"Hi, are you awake?"

I don't mind waking
in the middle of the night
to a thunderstorm.

Why think the rain sad?
It sings against my window,
dances in the air.

Wind whips through the elms,
scratches against the window,
blows the moon away.

It rained so gently,
Didn't even wake the birds.
Gave the trees a shine.

Distant hurricane
shaking the tambourine leaves.
Mist in the morning.

Seven-minute storm
left everything damp and blown.
Lighting over trees.

The soft morning light,
the rain that fell overnight,
the highway rumble.

Everyone's asleep.
They missed the wind blowing wild
and the sculptured clouds.

When I heard wolves howl,
I jumped straight out of my bed.
New cell phone ring tone.

Weekend sleeping in.
Something outside passes by,
Quiet as a book.

Mice, vole, kitty-cat,
plenty of good things to eat.
Urban coyote.

One more snooze alarm
gives in to the morning birds.
Snuggly sunny sheets.

The coffeepot calls:
An alarm for the morning
and the waking mind.

Warm peanut-butter
Oozing from the toasted bread.
Lick it from my hands.

Puffy water hands
slide the sponge against the cup.
My meditation.

Animal spirits
call on my inner otter,
my higher llama.

Vacation in time:
Let's go to 7 a.m.
and stay for a week.

Water soundly laps
on the shore, against the pier.
I'm singing along.

Waves rake the shore clean.
Sandy scent; water and peat.
Cyprus trees at home.

Cyprus trees rising;
they've been here for how long now?
Longer than the waves.

Lake of my childhood
shares its water with my eyes.
I don't want to leave.

It's not that time flies —
the days are long and restless —
it's that time has flown.

Days were pretty wild.
Finally sat down to read.
Finally sat down.

Orion surprise.
Already at steep angles
peeking through the trees.

Almonds and coffee,
Breakfast of astronomers,
Early moon risers.

Cloudy sky, no stars.
Cool mist dampens morning air.
Still, I'll stand outside.

Those threatening clouds,
wild like storms on Jupiter,
a few piddly drops.

Quiet time of day.
Everybody sleeps but me
and shushing highway.

Casting pagan runes.
Magic of the wayward mind.
Spell of the road trip.

On to the mountains;
then to the plains and prairies;
Stop at the ocean.

What is this wet land?
All the trees in soft focus.
Bone gray blur mist kiss.

Rolling ocean sighs,
here at the edge, gather those
who dare cross its waves.

I crossed the ocean.
It wouldn't be as much fun
without my wet feet.

Waves wash the island.
Anchor drops into the bay.
Rowboat to the shore.

I see Mount Fuji
sit in its perfect shadow.
Lie and close my eyes.

I see Mount Fuji.
I feel its cold morning rime
through my cotton shoes.

I see Mount Fuji
swarthed in clouds and foggy mist.
Eternal rainstorm.

The sky is clear there.
The bamboo sways in the breeze.
Mountain lodge fireplace.

Yes, I've been places.
Halfway around the green earth,
The rain smells like rain.

Returned from travels,
I came home to find my home
right where I left it.

Small house in the field.
One room is plenty for me.
Sun warms the water.

Cornfield waves its stalks.
Rabbits cut a path between,
highway in the dirt.

Heirloom apple tree,
who told you to grow that way?
Who plucks your lush fruit?

The rushing water,
drop by drop carved through these hills
to reach the calm pond.

Rocks in the water.
Water shushing over stone.
Silt and sand are born.

Dark water recess.
Treetops waving in the wind.
Whistle croak bark croak.

I was called upon
to open the wooden door
and let the night in.

Before the sunrise,
I stepped into the cool dark
and watched the moon set.

It looks so fragile,
that little sliver of moon
following Venus.

Dust falls from the sky,
screaming, burning to the earth.
Mad blaze; then it fades.

Four short shooting stars;
one unidentified flash;
and a string of geese.

Luxurious chill.
Standing outside in short sleeves
until I'm shaking.

This is the sweet spot.
I want to feel every day
of this September.

Little green stink bug.
I know it's cold out tonight.
You can stay inside.

Sunshine on the ground.
Leaves crunch as I walk to work.
Stiff grass shivering.

While I was at work,
Stink bug washed all the dishes.
OK, you can stay.

Hours before dawn,
night seems like a monolith.
Still. Still. Still. Still. Still.

Wakeful after dreams.
There's Jupiter and the moon.
Nightlight for writing.

As Saturn saunters,
I dream of ladies with rings
in rippling pale gowns.

Valleys of the moon,
light has reached your dusty floors,
warmed your lawless shores.

Surely there were seas
caroming the cratered shore,
clear and rolling tides.

If you look closely,
you will see the moon is full
really, all the time.

When sun kissed the moon,
she laughed at his ardent heat.
Then they danced all night.

Little green stink bug,
I have put the coffee on.
Let's read the paper.

Winter is coming,
though now it seems far away.
No more spiderwebs.

"Sweet! Sweet! Sweet!": the birds.
There aren't as many today.
Southern migration.

Bird says hi and yawns.
Can't tell if it's day or night.
When does the sun rise?

One lone bird singing,
confused by the rogue season.
"North today, or south?"

Inspiration flies
on the wings of simpler birds.
Practicality.

Sun that fills the moon
rises from the other side,
another night ends.

The sun has moved south,
spending the winter alone
in frosty gardens.

Don the warm wool coat.
Creaky hands with their dull ache
dodge into pockets.

Frosty-breath morning.
Stars are falling at my feet,
lighting ashen paths.

Twenty cops and me,
waking for the morning shift
with bacon and eggs.

Coffee wakes my nose.
Eggs for lasting energy.
Pancakes just for fun.

Autumn wonderland.
Cars swoosh by on wet streets,
sun sleepy like me.

Walking Quarry Park.
I find it better than books
for clearing the mind.

Stone of the quarry,
gray, rust-red, serrated walls,
the ages you've known.

Blue quarry water,
reflecting the sunny sky,
mirroring my mind.

Untroubled water,
reflecting rocks, trees and clouds.
Wish I were so still.

They're reaching so high!
Trees don't like saying goodbye
to the autumn sun.

Stacked cold river stone,
graced with smoke grass and black thorns.
I made you a shrine.

Still water meets rocks.
That's where the ripples begin.
Then there is music.

What did those trees say?
They're whispering all around,
throwing leaves at me.

Hey, I know these crows.
Here, friend, have a peanut.
What do you say now?

Dirt makes good pavement
for the trail to my castle.
Mud, a handy moat.

The leaves crumpled and fell.
You don't have to be in love
for your heart to break.

Wet leaves leave a trail,
deep into dark fertile woods,
feet silent on moss.

My quiet walk home.
I could almost hear the sun
playing with the clouds.

One red leaf still clings.
I know how to be lonely,
but not how to fall.

Hot tea, stack of books.
Candlelight colors the wall.
Winter night at home.

Sweet October night.
Open field of grass and stone.
A distant tractor.

Put out the candles.
Night is supposed to be dark.
Ghost and fox domain.

The moon is lazy;
rises later every night.
Time for a new one.

No one is richer
than backyard astronomers
sifting their diamonds.

Seven shades of blue
darken dusk with deeper hues,
punctuated by stars.

She wears a black gown
speckled with diamonds and pearls,
my lover, the night.

Swinging his bright sword,
Orion slices the sky.
Grumpy old uncle.

Planets have aligned,
tugging incrementally
at each other's hearts.

Galilean moons
Dancing in their broad courtyard
Outshine their sisters.

Seven sisters bathe
in a milky pool of haze,
naked and silky.

Seven sisters run
from the bull that chases them
through the morning sky.

While I watch the sky,
Saturn promenades across
in her gauzy skirt.

Swimming to Neptune,
light lost to depth, ice and smoke.
Chilly sea; blue sky.

Go ahead and laugh.
Uranus has heard your jokes,
still flies above you.

Sixteen shooting stars.
Sixteen wishes I have made,
all of them the same.

Sitting in the dark,
I peer as far as I can
into centuries.

Orion slinks home
after raging through the night,
followed by his dogs.

Walking by myself,
I found a perfect red leaf
to add to her shrine.

Beauty comes from scars,
imperfections, blemishes.
She, with her freckles.

A night walk downtown:
city lights, people and tea.
Conversation flows.

Unexpected guest.
The second cup for coffee
with clover honey.

I was up all night
memorizing every strand
of her soft brown hair.

Her berry-stained hands.
Her soft and furry places.
Her laughter, like chimes.

So we fell in love,
a thousand mattresses deep,
bright as the full moon.

Her unrestrained laugh.
Her skin, like soft cooling bread.
She is my deep sigh.

I'll never forget
through the tyranny of days
her delicate hands.

Winston-Salem native Mick Scott worked in the Winston-Salem Journal's editorial department for 20 years, the final five of those as editorial page editor. During that time, he churned out thousands of editorials and opinion columns on tight deadline and received numerous first- and second-place awards from the North Carolina Press Association. He's lived in four countries and visited 49 of the 50 states. He enjoys travel, reading, making art, and observing wildlife.

A collection of some of Mick's favorite Winston-Salem Journal opinion columns were published as *Stardust and Scar Tissue: Rambles, Ruminations, and the Search for an Authentic Culture of Life* in 2023 by Opine Press, an imprint of Press 53.

www.ingramcontent.com/pod-product-compliance
Lightning Source LLC
LaVergne TN
LVHW012022060526
838201LV00061B/4409